Specialness:
The Forbidden Fruit

POWERFUL NEW TEACHINGS FROM

"A COURSE IN MIRACLES"

Sharon Moriarty

GATEWAY TO ETERNITY PUBLICATIONS

http://www.GatewayToEternity.com

SPECIALNESS: THE FORBIDDEN FRUIT

Powerful New Teachings From

"A Course In Miracles"

Copyright © 2017 Sharon Moriarty

All rights reserved. No part of this book may be reproduced or transmitted in any form or by any means, electronic or mechanical, including photocopying, recording, or by any information storage and retrieval system without the written permission of the publisher, except where permitted by law.

ISBN (Paperback) : 978-0-9971179-7-4

LCCN : 2017913923

GATEWAY TO ETERNITY PUBLICATIONS

http://www.GatewayToEternity.com

SPECIALNESS: THE FORBIDDEN FRUIT

Preface: The Filter For Barflies 4

1. Specialness: The Forbidden Fruit 12
    The Myth of Our Superiority 27
    The Idol of Specialness 30
    Holiness, The Antidote For Specialness 40
    The Practice of Selflessness 42

2. Special Relationships 46
    The Dynamics of The Special Relationship 49
    Recognizing A Special Relationship 63

3. Radiant Thoughts 72
    1. Real Thoughts Never Vacillate in Their Message 75
    2. Real Thoughts Only Bring Joy 76
    3. Real Thoughts Empower and Liberate 78
    4. Real Thoughts Always Heal and Integrate the Mind 80
    Some More Examples of Real Thoughts 81

Author Bio 83

Other Books by Sharon Moriarty 84

PREFACE: THE FILTER FOR BARFLIES

The quest for meaning is probably the most powerful human drive. I know what you are thinking! That pleasure, sex, wealth, power, fame or even spiritual progress far surpass it in importance. Or that by gratifying and indulging the gates of the senses we can arrive at the temple of wisdom. However, bereft of meaningful purpose we rapidly become dull, enervated, and spiritless and wilt like overnight flowers.

Specialness: The Forbidden Fruit

Whenever our present embodies no meaning, we do not care for any future. The paths to bliss and meaning are the same because there is no lasting joy found in the meaningless. In contrast, once one has found a noble aspiration in which to channel their life vitalities, they become unconditionally joyous and immensely energized. The mystical poet William Blake wrote, "*Energy is Eternal Delight.*" He understood that the creative power of existence was energy, as it was bliss and this energy does not arise in a vacuum but ultimately derives from nurturing our divine capacities for reason and harnessing the wisdom of the soul.

You may have noticed, those boundless in energy are also incredibly creative and seemingly immune to disease. The rivers of their mind are always gushing to overflowing with ever new ideas and plans. Being spontaneous to life; they are fearless. It is not until the cup of our energy runs dry that we recognize its connection to eternal delight. All energy, physical, psychological and spiritual is a manifestation of Divine Creativity and follows automatically from following a supremely elevated and unambiguous sense of purpose. This enduring search is a natural and necessary drive since no can live for long without some higher function or goal. Look closely around, and you will recognize that those void of purpose are either overtly self-destructive or else they are listless, lifeless and scatterbrained.

I read this fascinating article recently about the hidden dangers of overdependence on workplace security. It chronicled the career paths of fully indentured Engineers, many of whom work their entire lives for large Government contractors, like Lockheed Martin. It blankly recounted how such Engineers, often die within a year or two of retiring. Why does this happen? It happens because we die once all sense of purpose has evaporated from our lives. We do not readily spot the dangers behind becoming overly conditioned and institutionalized. Our safety bubbles can become our greatest threat and death-traps unless on retirement we know how to redirect our energy and time. Many go through an inner meltdown and quickly crumple up even after a layoff. Having fallen from their pedestal of confidence, they degenerate into newborn babies that perpetually mope about the house; showering the airwaves with all sorts of redundant expletives. They resemble imbeciles and have lost all capacity to function.

Of course, this is no way to live, but it happens all the time. The modern lifestyle has poisoned us all with its sheepish vices of unquestioning complicity and security. Crazy Horse

Specialness: The Forbidden Fruit

would never have lived like this. Instead, heading it the battle of Little Bighorn, his catch cry was "*Hokahey! Today is a good day to die!*" One of the paradoxes of life is that only those willing to lose it can truly live!. Only those who remain open and courageous in the face of its upsets and daunting odds can taste its supreme fruit!

I remember this Engineering Manager from a long time back. He fascinated me simply because he was always so zealously inspired by his role leading a security equipment corporation. So one day, I visited him on site to see him in his niche. He was so impassioned about their capabilities and overall mission that his enthusiasm was contagious, if not evangelical (even to me who wouldn't normally care a toss.) Since he lived nearby, he brought me out for a nice lunch and a fine slew of pints, before I departed for the day.

I was somewhat shocked to hear, sometime later how he died from a heart attack, on the exact day he retired. Was this just chance or did his spirit instantly vacate the chambers once he perceived all sense of purpose as gone? Perhaps, the prospect of staring into the bleak hall of a humdrum existence, dusting off the furniture for his remaining years did not immediately appeal to him. What would he do except watch his body creak and groan and become increasingly more crocked! All while losing his mind to some invisible enemy behind the curtains. Likewise, we see how General George Patton did not last long once the theatre of WWII was no longer to command his energies. He passed on only a few months after VE day on Dec. 21st, 1945. The world is replete with tales and anecdotes like this, and they are not just urban legends, neither are they accidental or incidental. Most pass on immediately after their fundamental purpose is either complete or no longer relevant. We seriously oversimplify human motivations when we mistakenly think that it is food and shelter that keep us alive and healthy. There are higher psychological and spiritual forces at work that predominantly determine the scope and duration of our lives.

Meaningful purpose is perhaps the most critical psychological force in keeping us alive and enabling us to thrive. Didn't a great prophet once declare *"Man shall not live on Bread Alone."* We all know this to be true! We feel, most alive when we are in the process of accomplishing some great thing. It is in those moments of peak performance when we are operating in the zone, that our lives become a symphony of grace in motion. Then we operate flawlessly, and every cell and neuron in our bodies are synchronized and harmonized with the greater Source of life. Since our awareness is most acute and our actions so fluid, we feel invulnerable.

Specialness: The Forbidden Fruit

Many things we take for granted until they are there no more. Meaningful purpose is one of these things! Having a commendable purpose is what powers our existence. **It is the existential drug, we must have, or else we won't even be able to get out of bed and quickly perish.** Sadly many do not possess any higher or noble purpose, and so they compensate by adopting surrogate purposes that serve no holy, honorable or benign intention. The modern day ISIS warrior is a classical example of one who instigates all sorts of unholy atrocities in the name of justice and retribution. However, no one is fooled, and their brutal actions only mirror their unnatural desires for power at any cost and the unfillable void in their souls.

Some are unwilling to put in the effort to climb out of their self-made ghetto. These inertial beings are so tamasic in demeanor and negative in their outlook that they exude septic waves of poison into the surrounding spaces, sucking everyone down. You can call them psychic-vampires or bloodsuckers if you wish, or even the "**Army of the Dark Ones**," but we all know who they are, and of the crippling anti-energy, they unleash to all who come near. They are incorrigibly contractive, rather than expansive to life and to all possibilities it offers.

Most often they are incredibly fearful beings since a malignant paralyzing cancer has become deeply entrenched in their bones. They derive their only source of nourishment and comfort from sabotaging the dreams of others and extort great pleasure from dragging each into the mud and gutters of existence. Without any beacon of meaning to guide and energize them, they seek to enshrine the myth of their specialness and superiority above all other gods. Specialness is their supreme deity, as it is of all who cannot find any positive and altruistic purpose to their existence. Those who are quick to deride, castigate and besmirch the progressive elements in our societal fabric will be eager to fashion themselves into man-gods in their own private luniverses. Plagued and doomed by overpowering nightmares of their worthlessness they demand compensations on the worldly stage. Thus they attract sycophants, the world over, that will willingly prostrate before their feet and hand them the license over their minds and hearts.

This publication explores in detail our intense desire for specialness. It investigates what fuels and sustains this unholy need, and it threads unflinchingly into the many alluring forms our dreams of specialness take. You will learn the pernicious damage caused by this mind-bewitching idol which the ego needs for its survival. I will delve most lucidly into the

Course antidote for our specialness demands. An antidote which brings us in direct contact with the face of our innate holiness and the radiant and formless image of our original Creation. One suffused with the power to remove all distortions from our perception and so awaken our dreaming mind. I will probe courageously into the ego's most seductive temptation—that specialness safe-haven known as the **Special Relationships**. In particular, we will explore the unique attraction, toxicity and underlying dynamics by which Special Relationships operate and survive.

Thus, you will soon be an expert in unmasking all varieties of Special Relationship because, in content, they are one. You will comprehend the cursed dynamics by which they evolve to bait the witless and the tremendous cost each exacts. It is here, in these insidious nests of exclusion which serve as a bar to unconditional Love that the ego finds it most compelling means of salvation. It hopes you will accept its offering of illusionary love in place of your Reality and Immortal Grandeur.

1. Specialness: The Forbidden Fruit

> "It is essential to the preservation of the ego that you believe this specialness is not hell, but Heaven. For the ego would never have you see that separation could only be loss, being the one condition in which Heaven could not be."
>
> [ACIM, T-16.V.4:3-4]

In the movie, *"Amadeus,"* Mozart's contemporary, Antonio Salieri has dedicated his life to music. He desires the adulation of the masses and the accolade of being recognized as the greatest composer; the world has ever known. His one wish is to be honored forever for his sublime compositions. Unfortunately, he is soon overshadowed by the musical genius of Mozart. The effortless brilliance of this child prodigy exhibits Salieri's mediocrity to all. It is not long before bitterness sets in his heart, and he swears eternal revenge on God

Specialness: The Forbidden Fruit

for denying him the necessary talent. He becomes convinced that God is taunting and humiliating him through favoring this unmannerly brute, who laughs in his face and constantly ridicules him. Thus, he vows to destroy Mozart, with every breath, he takes. Yes, he will stomp this minion off the face of existence and succeed in murdering him. His crowning moment of glory will materialize through the performance of an exalted Requiem, to be played at Mozart's funeral. This heavenly composition will confer on Salieri, at last, the immortality he immensely craves. Since no one will know, he secretly commissioned it from Mozart; his revenge will be complete!

We see, however, that he is foiled in his ambitions. Soon all vestiges of his noble character, refinement and cultured sensibility disappear entirely. He becomes self-hating and destructive and eventually turns positively demonic. He locks himself in his room and starts cutting on himself. His great need for specialness has driven him insane. Finally, he is committed to a mental asylum, where he meets a priest who listens to his life story and confession. The engage in a somewhat adverse and confrontational dialogue which opens many past wounds. Nonetheless, all this probing into subconscious wounds and scars has a healing effect.

Salieri becomes capable of dropping his great specialness need and of establishing a loving connection with all those '"ordinary" and broken ones, that share the same asylum. This unseen hub of humanity, which he shunned before suddenly gain now his attention and compassion. He had always demanded the exceptional and extraordinary out of life, and this had blinded his eyes.

Demanding the world vindicate his dream of specialness, he could see nothing else. All who did not serve to uphold or champion it fell through his perceptual filters. Now recognizing his mistake, he begins to forgive to all these tortured souls. Almost immediately, the light, love, and joy which he had self-barred for decades streams back into his awareness. His forgiveness heals him of his specialness dream, and it restores vision. As, he glimpses the Face of his real Self and the incontestable spiritual bond he shared with all, he becomes truly grateful and appreciative.

Salieri's unique specialness pursuit and claim centered around music. Nevertheless, we all have peculiar specialness desires that keep us visionless. Our insatiable hankering after specialness always demands the sacrifice of others. Thus, we lose sight of our essential unity and witness only that world, which our twisted mind dreams allow. All else becomes screened, blocked or distorted. Specialness is the most alluring form of idol worship that the ego engages in. It is a kind of self-deification and a theme rampant throughout the world. As the Course teaches:

> **"The special ones are all asleep, surrounded by a world of loveliness they do not see. Freedom and peace and joy stand there, beside the bier on which they sleep, and call them to come forth and waken from their dream of death. Yet they hear nothing. They are lost in dreams of specialness."**
>
> [ACIM, T-24.III.7:1-4]

It is the elite crown, sought and prized by all egos and is universal, in nature because every ego feels the sting of the void and uses it to compensate for the tatters in its mortal dress. Once you recognize that the specialness demand is the invisible content lurking behinds all your dreams and aspirations, you will begin to see, how it is all-pervasive.

There are only a few genuinely humble beings. Even saints, in their endeavors, to increase their self-purity, often enter into quixotic battles with evil. Once evil is perceived as a real force to be reckoned with, its apparent reality then makes it extremely difficult to dispel. For one has then made the fatal mistake of making the unreal, real. Meaningful healing and purification can only follow from uncovering the light within. So does holiness become reflected everywhere! There never was a hostile engagement, because only one side of this conflict has ever been real. There is no real place for truth and illusion, to meet and wage war. Only a madman, deeply split within himself, who simultaneously endorses two antipodal systems of thought can believe this battlefield is real.

More extreme saints often embrace various forms of self-flagellation, deprivation, hardship, and torture to mitigate God's vengeance. Having unconsciously projected cruel intentions to their maker, they exact it first on themselves. Some monks have even undertaken self-mummification processes which are initiated half a dozen years before they pass.

Do they stop and ask why a God of unconditional Love would demand such nonsense? Why not join a local S&M club, take the lacerations there instead and transform yourself into a gimp in chains?

Specialness: The Forbidden Fruit

Why is the body being scapegoated, whipped, and brutalized for what is arbitrarily thought by the mind? Why not just attack a suit of clothes or take it out on a set of golf clubs! An approach, far less painful that accomplishes the same worthless goal. The crazy, senseless and insane activities, folk engage in, to extract an ounce of specialness, never ceases to mystify and confound me. Some will walk across Niagara on a tightrope, or fall 40km from space in a Billy Blastoff outfit just to gain some attention. Others prefer eating insects on *"Fear Factor,"* as their nutrition plan. Monkey brains and snakes apparently are not good enough to support their voracious spectrum of appetites. What some will do for the chance of winning $50k is astounding! Then we see all those mass murders at schools, movie theaters and churches that seem to attract a very niche subculture of the psychotic underworld. Most definitely, this is another specialness game that appeals to raving lunatics, in particular. However, anything less notorious cannot guarantee a five min media slot, or maybe even a T-Shirt.

Everyone needs some measure of specialness, weirdness, eccentricity or freakiness just to fit in. You must have your scars and stripes to enter the 21st century. All seek the priceless pearl of fame and notoriety or die trying. Now go out and market yourself and set some snares and bait, to lure some suckers in. Only then will these malleable doormats pay homage at your altar. Finding someone with no specialness demand is itself exquisite. For one, perfectly content to be considered ordinary is rare indeed. Those ready to celebrate their existence and being without any strings, extend a silent blessing to us all. They honor their Creator because they have accepted His Masterwork, as one of perfection. Seeking no honors or distinctions, and harboring no false pretensions is the "special" magic, that sets them apart. By recognizing and embracing the miraculous in what seems ordinary, they become extraordinary. It is only needy, lost and empty souls who seek for additional bells and whistles. These will insist that the world compromise and adjust to their design. Such special ones are utterly mundane and blasé and relentless attention grabbers and beggars on the face of existence.

The few, who are willing to dismantle all ego erected barriers of specialness and separation bring the gift of healing to all. They help purge our **One-Mind,** we all share of all redundant impediments to communication. They eliminate all illusory disconnects that only serve to isolate and further alienate. So doing, they restore back awareness of our ever-present unity. In consequence miracles and miraculous thinking patterns become natural again because the unimpeded and pure mind

Specialness: The Forbidden Fruit

is spontaneous and in harmony with the Creative Power of the Divine.

Presently, a return to our primitive past is currently *en vogue*. The airwaves blast us nightly with new images of some nude pygmies regressing back to their caveman selves, for a period of twenty-one days. Such is the Colosseum of the modern era, and we enjoy seeing these young ones shivering in their birthday suits getting ready for some serious, dehydration and kidney damage, all from the comfort of our living rooms. They require the specialness accolade of possessing expert survivorship skills.

On the first British expedition to Everest, George Mallory was probed on just why he wished to climb it. His only response was, "*Because it's there.*" Not a very good answer! More that of an impetuous schoolboy, naïve to all dangers who yet insists on taking senseless and unproductive risks. Mallory's body lay buried on the mountain for seventy-five years before being discovered. Some, in their vanity, try swimming the Antarctic while others eagerly engage in extreme missions, which offer little hope of survival. It seems even self-annihilation is not a big enough price to pay for our dreams of self-aggrandizement.

All the same, when we scrutinize these endeavors, we cannot ignore the glaring fact that they are all ultimately pointless. All they ever accomplish is to inspire another million egos to chase after the same vain and idle pursuits. They do nothing to end world poverty and suffering nor do they usher in a realm pervaded by genuine progress and peace. There is no doubt that Olympians are dedicated and passionate in their pursuit of Olympic glory. They train rigorously for years, in the hope of racking up some gold medals, to place around their necks. Then they stand in supreme silence for a few minutes, sporting a serene glow, as they listen proudly to their national anthem being recited. But beneath this pompous facade, there is a menacing voice that clamors and roars, *"See, I am far better than all of you guys."* Some go home to rack up a number DUIs while others pee their way back to the Olympic village. All speedily fall from their pedestal of eminence, and within a few short years, the shrine of their bodies has become a dilapidated house in an embarrassing state of disrepair. Similarly, the luniversities are flooded with researchers and professors earning multiple PhDs in meaningless fields. Most are stuffy, arrogant and conceited fools, who write research papers ad nauseam and file patent after patent. They will gladly burn the midnight oil, a thousand times over, if only it will lend them that extra ounce of specialness, in the eyes of their peers.

Specialness: The Forbidden Fruit

Business tycoons like to pride themselves on their entrepreneurial success and capacities for innovation. They adopt divide-and-conquer tactics and willingly consent to slash the livelihoods of thousands if only to get their names in the paper. They feel compelled to do something drastic to justify their excessive compensation and perks. And they crave that specialness dream of being seen as an original, cutting edge and powerfully dynamic reorganizational guru. Next day the stock price fluctuates, a tad, but their enduring legacy is that of having ruined the lives of many. Those pushed out, often enter vicious cycles of debt from which they never recover. Another Humpty Dumpty who has fallen off the wall never to work again. After a few years, they become too dispirited to search and drop into that cynical and disillusioned army of the chronically unemployed. The industry leader's first instinct is to destroy their competition. Reason and collective interest would indicate that it is far better to coexist symbiotically and for the common good. Coexistence ensures new ideas keep streaming in and it also forces a business to remain agile, competitive and efficient. We all know what happens when monopolies are allowed to thrive unchecked. The cable companies are one classic example. The lack of competition over the last decade has enabled them to skyrocket their costs for services. Meanwhile, their customer service has never been worse.

Nature can teach us plenty because whenever parts of an ecosystem are allowed to become extinct, the integral structure rapidly collapses. After a while, large clusters of animal and plant life start dying out and soon the entire spectrum of diversity with all its broad relationships and critical linkages can decidedly contract.

The intense craving for specialness is out of control in the media and entertainment industries. Let's face it, Hollywood is nothing but a vanity club of Cyclopean proportions. A glorious meat market that relentlessly showpieces a vast smorgasbord of hot and fashionable bodies. All eye candy upon which we feast. This exotic marketplace is filled to the brim with pumped up chickens, anorexic females, boob and body jobs, Botox injections, butchered surgeries, dens of iniquity and various enclaves for shameless intoxication and pleasure seeking. Let's not forget, for a moment all the leeches, parasites, groupies and fanatics, that fervently follow the scent. In short, it is a Boris Karloff freak-show on steroids where overly glossed lipstick queens and ostentatious icons go prancing around in their expensive rags and hairdos, for a night. All seeking to vaunt and flaunt the icy veneer of their specialness before the world. Next day, the slippers come off, and the halo disappears, and we hear juicy stories of how they were lynched in their driveways and carted off for their

DUI mugshots. Even so, this haze of phoniness and superficial pomp has so drugged and sedated our minds that we begin to hate our immensely monotonous, plebian, and soul-crushing lives. We fool ourselves into fantasizing that there is still some glamor left in this mephitic cesspit of sweat and mangled bodies, all clambering to get to the light first. But this is not the mystical mist which leads to the Orphic Buddhaverses and Kingdoms of inner peace.

The all-consuming need for specialness is the treacherous virus infecting the human psyche. It is an airborne pathogen, flagrant and uncontrolled and capricious in its whims. From the ghettos to the prison systems to the technology-brain-farms and the red carpets, all bow down before and apotheosize the gods of specialness. We even smell its insidious presence lurking in the geek, freak, misfit, and vagabond subcultures. All go around bug-eyed, entranced by their plastic toys. Now and then they spontaneously cachinnate intense bursts of some indecipherable nonsense, communicated in a cryptic Nexus 6 lingo that none of us can crack.

Our prisoners like to spend their days painting stripes and flying kites. They have come to represent a new breed of genetically engineered animals specially produced by our institutions and healing sanctuaries of correction. The meal plan must have been low in protein for them to turn so carnivorous, on one another. But hey it is a great place to throw out your business card and build up your network of gang affiliations. Perhaps you can speckle your resume with Sureños and Norteños and maybe the odd member of the Aryan Brotherhood. Then have contacts for life. Naturally, they take great pride in their powers of invention, deception, and ingenuity even if restricted to Barney Rubble forms of communication. Perhaps if you are class enough, you will become the Shank Kai-Chek of the prison yard. The spectrum of specialness has its pinnacle with the serial killers, who get the highest marks on the food chain. Sadly it is all downhill from there. All the way down that slippery slope to the perverts and child molesters, at the bottom.

Evidently, our specialness need is class independent, and it can even ascend the ladder into the spiritual domains. Thus, in recent years, we have witnessed an explosive growth market in spiritual materialism. The merchandising of false prophets in rampant now in every online cubbyhole. A dazzling and splendiferous array of charlatans, con artists, and diviners has arisen overnight pandering to the unhealthy projections of their followers. Such adulators, groupies, and New Age minions being inherently weak, naturally seek self-validation from without. All are supremely malleable un-

Specialness: The Forbidden Fruit

thinking beings. Pliant pre-programmed goons of the spiritual variety, just waiting to be branded and brainwashed. Curiously restless to dedicate themselves to the wooden totem pole of some prophet of the New World Order. They will willingly sign over their life savings and the lease on their coconut if only another will absolve them of all responsibilities and replace these instead with some special mantra for salvation. As expected, such organizations do not deliver any lasting transformation. They merely provide psychic-bandaids which temporarily cover gaping holes in the self-concept of the weak and delusional.

"How bitterly does everyone tied to this world defend the specialness he wants to be the truth! His wish is law to him, and he obeys. Nothing his specialness demands does he withhold. Nothing it needs does he deny to what he loves. And while it calls to him he hears no other Voice. No effort is too great, no cost too much, no price too dear to save his specialness from the least slight, the tiniest attack, the whispered doubt, the hint of

threat, or anything but deepest reverence. This is your son, beloved of you as you are to your Father. Yet it stands in place of your creations, who *are* son to you, that you might share the Fatherhood of God, not snatch it from Him."

[ACIM, T-24.VII.1:1-8]

THE MYTH OF OUR SUPERIORITY

We are all born with the thinly veiled belief that we are extraordinary and unique in some worthwhile way. Far superior to the throng of troglodytes, we see around us. This unsubstantiated madness, we savagely protect and shield from every possible assault. Thus we erect an extensive array of defenses around ourselves to serve as shelters from an invasive world. Many of these defenses are aggressive by design such as **judgment, attack, condemnation, and projection.**

Others are crafted ingeniously! and this enumeration includes **denial, dissociation, and temporization.** Alternatively, we may choose to be passively hostile, aloof or evasive or introduce smoke screens and maelstroms of confusion. We leverage and augment ourselves through secretly ridiculing others from the safety and privacy of our bubble worlds. All our defenses aim to establish some distance between us and the world, and they thwart all hopes of authentic communication.

> "**What else could justify attack? For who could hate someone whose Self is his, and Whom he**

knows? Only the special could have enemies, for they are different and not the same. And difference of any kind imposes orders of reality, and a need to judge that cannot be escaped."

[ACIM, T-24.I.3:3-6]

"Could you attack your brother if you chose to see no specialness of any kind between you and him?"

[ACIM, T-24.I.7:7]

As soon as any of our core defenses are perforated, we immediately scrunch up like a wounded animal and become outright vicious. Our lack of specialness can never be exposed because this is the towering differentiator separating gods and men. Hence, we enthusiastically scavenge the world of perception for all that serves to reinforce our belief system. We do not care if our actions involve mercilessly cutting the legs out from under another. Likewise, we stealthily avoid all who can exercise psychological leverage over us and attempt to forge special relationships with the more powerful since this can add more jewels to our crown.

The Idol of Specialness

The idol of our specialness increases our sense of separation, and it provides immense motivation for sniffing out all sorts of lurid sins and attractive failures in others. The myth of our specialness demands fresh blood and survives through holding intractable beliefs in sin and inferiority. Sin is used as a comparative device to separate the worthy from the worthless. Meanwhile, the blind eyes of our specialness search for every lack, deficiency, cruelty or vice, which it can use to crucify without mercy. All failures, weaknesses or flaws are carefully cataloged and stored away in its prodigious memory. It seeks to enshrine all mistakes or flaws into irredeemable sins because sin is sacred to the ego. Over time these become impenetrable barriers to forgiveness and protect the dream of our specialness.

The ego carves out its entire existence from illusion, and it masterfully deploys the mythical tale of our specialness to cover the true Reality of others. By besmirching and traducing all, it hopes to gain in stature. Mockery, ridicule, hostility, and grandiosity are some of the tools that it uses most strategically in this malicious pursuit.

Specialness: The Forbidden Fruit

To paraphrase Shakespeare, "Specialness is like **the green-eyed monster which doth mock the meat it feeds on.**" So we live behind masks and only ever present tattered illusions of ourselves. Our Radiant Identities go unknown for they can never communicate through the superficial veneer afforded by our masks.

Where specialness is esteemed, the altar to Truth goes unseen and unheard because an impossible dream has become reified, sanctioned and glorified in its place. This ego seduction denies us Heaven, and it has caused, **"the Once Mighty,"** to have fallen far from grace. In fact, all the way from our divine sovereignty into the vapid pools of longstanding mediocrity. But such is the fate of all those who gladly embrace the ego's tiny meretricious gift of specialness in place of their majesty, immortality and Divine Grandeur. When we strive after notoriety, praise or worldly esteem in any form, we remain unaware of our innate perfection. Illusions are powerless to add to our value because we remain, as always, unified with the Source of all Creative Power. Specialness must exclude because it demands the throne for itself. Not wishing to share the Kingdom, it has deprived us of it. Our endless obsession with gaining false distinctions and flimsy merits dim all awareness of our underlying unity.

The "**special**" all live in their private bubbles that are fragile and powerless and ready to go splash at any instant. Hermetically sealed off from their real source of strength, they live a whimsical, unstable and soul-starved existence. Like waves crashing against the shoreline, they foolishly imagine that they are separate, autonomous and independent from the vast ocean of Mind. Not recognizing the sea of tranquility in which they are seamlessly merged, they cannot leverage its power. The outer altar to specialness is the body, but the mind is its host because our thoughts alone are the fuel that nourishes it. In specialness, the ego sees salvation, for, in this resplendent idol, it finally thinks it can complete itself. Nonetheless, all hopes of attaining self-completion through exclusion must fail because this is the one condition in which all vision becomes blocked, miracles barred and holiness unknown.

> **"Here are the gates of hell you closed upon yourself, to rule in madness and in loneliness your special kingdom, apart from God, away from truth and from salvation."**
>
> [ACIM, T-24.II.13:4]

Specialness is not the dream that frees but one that further isolates and imprisons. It instantiates a fantasy kingdom into your mind which has no witnesses and can never be made true. Because of its insecure foundation, it must shake tremulously with every breeze that blows. In this hostile world, you wander about like a mangy dog across a lonely, barren and frozen landscape, feeling under constant threat from everything that moves. Nonetheless, the ego will never admit to failure nor declare this senseless dream is taking the place of your Inheritance.

"It is your specialness that is attacked by everything that walks and breathes, or creeps or crawls, or even lives at all. Nothing is safe from its attack, and it is safe from nothing."

[ACIM, T-24.III.4:4-5]

The fearful and downtrodden are unlikely to have any residual memory of their indisputable divinity. Instead, stalking the earth, tacky and disheveled, they image grotesque homunculi in their broken down frames. Even so, their stuffy, pretentious airs and grandiosity go undiminished and relentless in their beggar-hood for more. Nor can they admit that their deceitful wish has left them bankrupt. For specialness, in its unholy desire to extract all life-juices, fatally blinds to the vision of holiness.

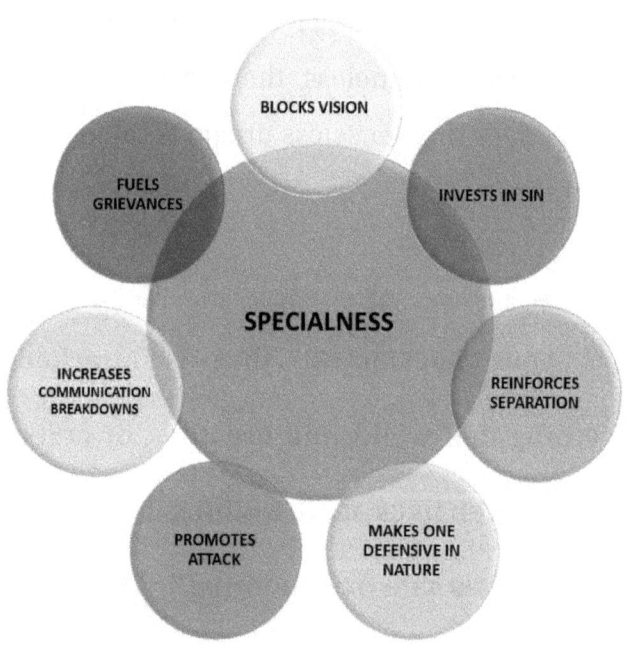

SOME OF THE PROBLEMS INTRODUCED BY THE WISH FOR SPECIALNESS

The diagram above portrays some of the consequences of our specialness desire. It is evident that it affects every aspect of our world experience. Additionally, it unleashes myriad pernicious influences which tarnish and shatter our psychological makeup. This depiction is just a slice of its real cost. Specialness propagates fear since it calls for increased isolation and alienation.

Through this wish, we become frozen off into our self-made dungeons where an abundance of unneeded defenses and excessive armature seem necessary for our continued protection. Since vision becomes denied, we descend further into dark dreams. Thus our grievances only increase. As we become more embittered, viperous and fearful, our faith becomes sealed.

> **"Here does the Son of God ask not too much, but far too little. He would sacrifice his own identity with everything, to find a little treasure of his own. And this he cannot do without a sense of isolation, loss and loneliness."**
>
> [ACIM, T-26.VII.11:7-9]

Specialness is the ego's most cherished idol. The special glue by which egos join to make alliances or fragment to initiate tribal warfare. The ego uses the myth of our specialness to justify all barriers it erects. Each ego perceives itself as sole architect of reality and as Master of its destiny. Egos collectively join for what they can individually plunder; not for what they can cede or award. There can be no real solidarity among egos, ever. As soon as there is nothing more to gain, the relationship turns sour and is then shunned, abandoned and forgotten.

This desire for specialness takes many forms. It can be recognized in our voracious needs to be esteemed as more intelligent, crafty, beautiful, noble, classy, colorful, or refined. Our particular fantasy is often something very sublime, challenging, difficult to accomplish or well beyond reach. If one has no exceptional talents to satiate their specialness craving, they will carve it out in other ingenious ways. Maybe by being overly gross, doing something daring or persevering or by defrauding others in a Ponzi scheme. Being average is to be avoided at all costs. Mediocrity is the immortal enemy of specialness. It gives one the scent of a low-life skunk in the human pond. Each moment the ego frantically searches for ever new bonds to forge and others to dismantle. In the hysteria that follows, one becomes far more obsessed with what is going on outside than in their indigenous thought. Very sensitive then to how many new connections they have on Twitter, Facebook, Instagram and the like. An invisible covenant is locked in between all parties which tacitly declares:

> **"I will support your particular dream of specialness, so long as you support mine."**

This thinly veiled agreement forms the basis of all special relationships. The world is a never-ending hub of insincerity, psychological warfare, fleeting patterns, and counterfeit ideals. A virtual arena where a contagion of competing egos fight to the death for the most trivial things. It offers no stability, dependability or mercy because circumstances and motivations are always changing in the ego world. Consequently, the ego itches for all forms of security it can garner from this maelstrom of madness. Be very careful then, of what you are endorsing on the dotted line and of all that lies hidden in the fine print. Each ego contract goes something like this:

"I want to extract all, of value in you and make it my own. I seek to plunder the jewel in your heart and the totality of your wisdom and insights. If I need to spill a few pints of your blood onto

the tarmac in the process and take out your kidneys too, all the better. First I will wear you as an ornament around my neck and put you into my display case to parade before others. Finally, I will exhibit your mutilated carcass around town as my show dummy before speedily discarding you to the trash."

Yes, every breach of the contract must be paid for in blood. Then as you slump there, half conscious, barely clinging for life, you find the ego's ravenous and savage appetite only momentarily appeased. It cruelly states:

"Whenever you fail to support my chosen dream, I will project the failing cause to you. Thus, is my rage justified! Your continued inadequacy, deficiencies and utter lack of competency or merit place our collective dream of salvation on a very slippery foundation. Hence, if I objurgate you mildly or spout out some random calculated insults among the crowd, know they are well deserved. A mere cracking of my whip to get your attention while demonstrating my power and leverage over you."

The ego always follows up with some false displays of forgiveness and insincere reconciliation. But cooking below is the bubbling cauldron of all the personal slights and tragedies it has ever suffered. The atonement of which demands vengeance. Often the ego will rapidly reappear in all its naked

Specialness: The Forbidden Fruit

wickedness and glory. Mindlessly ranting that "*It is Showtime baby*," as it spirals into a degenerative meltdown that is positively maniacal and Satanic. This miserable cacophony of fuming fury and abject mindlessness may even be construed as catatonic to the initiated. In any case, it has sworn another lifelong enemy with whom to share another special hate relationship. Soon, it rapidly incarnates into a God of cruelty. One hell-bent on destroying all dreams and burning you on the worldly stage for all to see. Now, is the bleak content lurking in all its ideologies and false gifts seen up close and personal! It will never admit to how it tried to use you, nor hint at any chink or vulnerability in its armor. It carefully conceals all its malicious intentions, for it desires you serve out a life sentence as a trophy to itself.

But you punk came up short! You broke the invisible and sacred covenant of trust, and are therefore a flatfish with zero integrity. Now that the deceptive phase of the relationship is over, the death spiral begins. Two reptiles toss and turn in the filth each trying to get in the killer bite. Such is the naked reality of each special relationship experienced at its core.

HOLINESS, THE ANTIDOTE FOR SPECIALNESS

The choice to recognize Holiness remains our one real alternative to wallowing in futile dreams of specialness. This recognition requires forgiveness to undo all the damage and distortion inflicted through our judgments and myths of superiority. Quantum forgiveness brings forth the vision in which we witness the eternal flame of spirit in all! That beacon of effulgent brilliance that remains forever quiet and powerful, and serenely unmoved by all our wild delusions of specialness. Our original Mind is immaculate and forever unchanged by time and illusion. It exists like a blank slate, or pure Tabula Rasa, to which no unrealities can ever cling. This Holy Mirror is free of the dust induced by memory, imagination, fantasy, and fear.

Truth can never enter our dreams. Nonetheless, it lies hidden beneath all the false analytic overlay and subterfuge generated by our lower mind. As we relinquish, those sporadic, calculating, nonsense thoughts of our egos, our holiness becomes reflected everywhere. Then we become aware of our everlasting invulnerability, perfection, and wholeness. Vision is the gift that keeps on giving for it enables the "**Great Rays**" to extend outward so that we can recognize the One Self in all. It is through this awareness alone that we can heal, cure and integrate our minds.

Specialness, in contrast, works to impede this light, and so it serves to keep us hostage to dreams of sickness, suffering, blindness and prolonged isolation. This Trojan horse we welcomed so warmly behind our gates is what deceives us entirely. For its mission is to uphold illusions, not to dismantle them. Judgment perceives qualitative differences that are fleeting and chimerical by nature while Holiness merely advocates on behalf of Truth. It knows there can be no differences in what is forever One and teaches how Oneness is our life and strength. The belief in differences is what propagates fear.

Holiness brings in its wake unassailable peace and remembrance of unconditional Love. Specialness, in contraposition, freezes us into self-made hells where fear alone reigns supreme. In these demonic realms, we feel alienated, and haunted by shadows and trapped in a perpetual state of dread and anxiety.

THE PRACTICE OF SELFLESSNESS

From an early age, we are taught to be selfish and to take whatever we can, most mercilessly. Sure! The mask of cultivated civility is there too, so parents advise their children to be considerate of the needs of others, but secretly they want them to thrive and to compete at all costs to win. Second place is not good enough because they desire their offspring rise well above the class of mediocrities in which they find themselves endlessly floundering. Thus, they reward their children for any merits and distinctions they accomplish and eagerly sign them up on all sorts of extracurricular programs for the gifted.

Is it a surprise then, when we glance around, we see this selfish gene evidenced everywhere? All the vanity clubs and throngs on social media taking selfies of everything they do from picking their nose to going for a latte. You may think that the opposite of selfishness is selflessness, but nothing could be further from the truth. Selflessness, properly understood involves the obliteration of the false, superficial social self so that your real Immaculate Self can shine.

The Buddhist Masters employ the practice of selflessness to restore back our natural, original and holistic awareness. This undefiled awareness alone is capable of mirroring the Real. Selflessness overcomes the poison of attachment which then removes a critical foothold by which the ego clings for survival. Buddhism does not emphasize God since they understand how the relative mind sustains itself and grows through idol worship. They articulate and emphasize the notion of **the Void** to foil all efforts the mind undertakes to twist the eternal into yet another phenomenal conception. In the Void, all concepts and forms are annihilated and disappear. This path of selflessness cleanses one's eyes of all defilements and cataracts placed on them by the ego. By suctioning out all wind from the sails of its pernicious ideologies, they rid you of the ego for good. As a consequence, the indestructible and formless Truth of never-ending Life, Love, and Bliss becomes once again evident.

Selflessness is one of the fastest paths to Self-Liberation, for it offers a very humble, direct and guaranteed passage into the Buddhaverse of Nirvana. It should not be mistakenly construed as a practice of self-diminishment or self-effacement since its noble goal is Self-recognition. A goal it accomplishes through rigorously purging all erroneous beliefs you have garnered from living within the relative realm.

The idol of specialness chains you to unnecessary bondage and suffering, and it delays your healing and joy. It introduces endless artificial barriers which seem to separate you from the great ocean of Being. Only by merging with the non-differentiated space of Nirvana, can you know of your infinite potency and essential deathlessness! For you are that indestructible, timeless awareness that is non-grasping, pure and impartial by nature. You Real Self is like a holy mirror, to which no illusions can ever cling. You Are the formless creative awareness in which all things appear to happen. As you reach the exalted state of Buddha consciousness, known as *Bodhicitta,* you put out the flame. Your awareness and creativity go on, but the impurity of the phenomenal, relative, and time-bound existence is snuffed out for good. Hence, the symbolic flame is a metaphor for relinquishing the phenomenal world, in a mesmerizing bonfire of illusion. The phenomenal is a phantasmagoric empire built from all your limiting concepts and mistaken beliefs.

The practice of *no-self* brings you into the presence of your Authentic Self. This bubble bursting technique dissolves all superficial barriers to your Totality. As you become one with the formless and undifferentiated, the noumenal backdrop reappears from the mists. The noumenal is that potent, unmanifest and abstract Kingdom that became lost in your dreams of ignorance. Since the Samsaric experience and mind-frame has been extinguished, the natural illumination of Immaculate Mind alone shines in a cloudless sky. Now you are awakened, and all dreaming has ended.

2. SPECIAL RELATIONSHIPS

The phases of each special relationship are similar to the four stages of death. Except it goes more like this: **(i) Denial (ii) Anger (iii) Depression/Despair** and **(iv) Alienation.**

Denial that you are not the perfect solution for all my cruel intentions and unrealistic expectations. So instead, I will hold a radiant and glowing image of you and temporarily deny all your flaws. **Anger** and rage set in conclusively, as your failure to meet all my needs and ideals, becomes glaringly indisputable. I find, to my dismay that I cannot exploit or manipulate you as I wish. I become **depressed**, that I am stuck with a born loser, who is of no use. The terrifying thought that I may have to support you for the rest of my life or myself torments me endlessly. I am even embarrassed now to be spotted with you in public. So, I hide behind my laptop or distract myself on my smartphone.

Beyond closed doors, we are similar to two demons or psychic-vampires and endlessly lock horns. I find myself in despair for being caught in this rat-hole of a relationship; One

Specialness: The Forbidden Fruit

that has become cemented with kids. However, my escape from it may turn out to be very costly indeed. I need to do something pronto, to break it up; something to justify all my attacks and petty recriminations. I vow to use every means possible to isolate and **alienate** you further so that our life together will be more glacial than that of Frosty the Snowman. I will ridicule and dehumanize at every opportunity and extract delight in pushing all your buttons until finally, you cave and appear to leave of your own accord. Alternatively, you may have entered a special relationship with the purpose of self-glorification through another's wealth or connections. So starts the phase of **Denial**! Unfortunately, you are finding out now that the "special one" that so attracted is in reality, a prescription junky, chronic gambler or out-of-control alcoholic. Or maybe they are a shopaholic or selfaholic instead — does it make a difference?

Anger sets it, as you recognize the full extent of your self-deception. One you chose to ignore in pursuit of an unrealizable fantasy. Why were your so blind for so long? You had rationalized excessively and foolishly believed your myopic distortions of intent played no part in your original deception. Now you are so far down the rabbit hole that any hope of finding a progressive or self-redeeming way out seems a hopeless misadventure.

For a long while, you oscillate between anger and denial. Chronically frustrated you subconsciously repress the symptoms at times or search for tacky workarounds to avoid facing some of the pain and core issues. You want to cut your losses now and conceive that there may be some jewels or nuggets of value worth rescuing from this relationship. Perhaps the unwanted elements and aspects can be simply ignored or discarded and placed to the side of your plate.

Soon **depression** sinks in, as you fully realize, the hook is in far too deep. Your self-anger escalates at your deception. This other is a lunatic on the loose, and he or she is going to sink the both of you. Now the guilt trips and threats begin to gain momentum. You glimpse the full extent of how you are going to be sabotaged and taken apart wing-for-wing when trying to escape it. For a while, you sit there hopeless and resigned like an insect trapped in a spider's web. Awaiting your cruel faith of being eaten alive. **Despair** is all you can feel now as you surmise the world through Shawshank eyes. You no longer dare to hope, knowing hope is a dangerous thing. Even a shred of hope now is an overly optimistic prospect; An intangible that presents a perfect storm to your disgruntled conscience.

THE DYNAMICS OF THE SPECIAL RELATIONSHIP

Definite core dynamics unfold in each special relationship. Firstly, there the idol of illusionary love, at its center. In this endeavor, one projects perfection to another. Since this other now engenders all hope of attaining self-completion, they are idolized and worshiped as a god. Nonetheless, such love is aberrational because in your love induced state of blindness you ignore all their flaws. You demand that they be only, what your arbitrary fantasies would make of them.

Hypnotized by the spell of your love intoxication, you would gladly reprogram the whole universe of thought and twist the entire matrix of perception on its heels, to accomplish your special love dream. Meanwhile, Love's real face goes unknown. It cannot be known where there is a beggary of passion and the mind stupefying haze of self-delusion. Soon, however, your eyes are opened, as the evidence mounts that this particular love bubble of illusion is going to burst. Infallibilities are now seen as glaring weaknesses, unvanquishable altruism as self-obsession, kindness as camouflaged opportunism, and beneath the stunning portrait of beauty and innocence lies the dark imprint of the Antichrist. At this stark juncture, your special love relationship has transmogrified into one of special hate. In essence, they are the same for they build from the same cursed psycho-mechanics. Only on the surface, do they appear different! In the final analysis, your ego needs for security, self-fulfillment, and self-preservation drives both types of relationship. It strategically uses the special love relationship as a ploy to avoid admitting its personal lack of specialness, because this is a truth too harsh to bear. So it projects love and specialness to another, in the hopes that its individual deficiencies can be temporarily overlooked.

The ego can tolerate almost anything except being perceived as ordinary, and it conceives exalting another is the way to escape this. It would prefer, to be regarded as a crazed lunatic or serial killer than to be seen as so utterly traditional, commonplace and bourgeois in its attitude and approach. It craves the inflated self-concept that special love brings even though it arises out of distortion and is merely a projection of its narcissistic tendencies. Each special love relationship has its roots in projected narcissism. Once, it fails, the ego regroups and makes every attempt to save face. It hopes to recover its losses quickly by engaging in new affairs.

Nevertheless, all are doomed because they operate under the same ill-fated mechanics. The hope of finding Love, in any specialness relationship is an unachievable goal because true Love can never be exclusionary.

> **"In Heaven, where the meaning of love is known, love is the same as union. Here, where the illusion of love is accepted in love's place, love is perceived as separation and exclusion."**
>
> [ACIM, T-16.V.3:7-8]

Each special relationship is an attempt to manufacture love through fragmentation and exclusion while denying underlying unity and Oneness. Each seeks to grasp the benediction of Love while still retaining exceptions. Such relationships cannot even embrace a single individual in their totality but only those aspects that are to one's immediate liking. The Holy Spirit, in contrast, teaches the lack of exceptions is the lesson because whenever you hold exceptions, Love remains unknown. Complete inclusion is the one condition in which the Kingdom, is remembered.

"I call upon you to remember that I have chosen you to teach the Kingdom *to* the Kingdom. There are no exceptions to this lesson, because the lack of exceptions *is* the lesson."

[ACIM, T-7.XI.4:1-2]

Special relationships are primarily concerned with the most external and superficial characteristics of another. It is this alone they aim to glorify while callously ignoring the nefarious intentions that motivate and underlie them. They never desire you to embrace the authentic Reality of another. So, in the end, you may end up traveling a million provocative worlds and exploring a gazillion different exotic relationships and never find a thing.

The Holy Spirit takes you on a voyage that uncovers the true Source of love within yourself. He strives to smash through all fortifications and defenses the ego has interposed against Love. Only so, does the ego world come crashing down, and you begin to witness miracles of Love instead. On this holy voyage, you become non-judgmental and forgiving and walk the path of gratitude. You begin to shower blessings and kindness on all while relinquishing your petty games of control and manipulation. Likewise, you terminate all your ego schemes of parasitically feeding off another's attention and merits. The special relationship is Love's opposite in every way. It is a content of fear and hate framed in a form that seems loving and represents the ego's chosen shabby substitute for Love; its attempt to bring Love into separation. All the ego can ever manage to do is to produce the illusion of love. The variability of love in the special relationship and the vicious psychodramas that play out in it highlight its unreality. Real Love can be depended upon always. It does not lessen or weaken with time, nor is it derailed by idols and extraneous influences. It is not subject to contingency nor the vacillations of the marketplace. Nothing can diminish its power and quiet certitude. Being limitless, ever potent and whole its joy is in gratefully extending itself freely to all while demanding nothing in return.

Does the special relationship exhibit such characteristics, or does it come with so much unnecessary baggage and conditions? Perhaps also some temper-tantrums and acrimony on occasion? The special relationship is associated with a loss of freedom, power, and self-esteem. Feelings of irritability, confusion, anxiety, sacrifice, hate, disillusionment, depression, guilt, fear, and despair all arise within its bleak manifold! All of which becomes inevitable when you deny the Source of Love within and seek for it externally.

Your motives were suspect from the start. You had devalued yourself and schemed to rob another to fill that void in your soul. You were attempting to purchase the illusion of love by sacrificing yourself at an alien altar. You felt you were appeasing the god of love, whom you saw as demanding sacrifices. So you had deemed yourself worthless and raised another onto the pedestal as a private gift to yourself. Both stand now as symbols for a botched attempt to substitute for Love's reality within.

If you could simply have embraced the other wholly and in perfect faith, the way to Love would have been easy and sure. Then they would have served as a perfect reflector of the truth of Love within and everywhere. You decimated the real meaning of Love when you introduced exceptions and exceptional people. That endless search for compromises, bargains, and contingencies which the ego commands bars all meaning from all relationships. It defines their bounds and limitations and establishes just how far you are willing to go in the game of sacrifice.

Specialness: The Forbidden Fruit

All who enter into special relationship come with their shades of gray. There are tacit words unspoken of just how much is expected so that your ego cravings for love and specialness can be fulfilled.

Thus, you have a fondness for your lover's eyes, but not her ears, you like her behind but not her fat belly. You feel her pot belly and nose protrude a little too far or that her voice squeaks or croaks incessantly like a frog. You see her, at times, as caring and considerate but then complain that she is not adventurous enough. Oh yes, she has imagination, flamboyance and many fanciful notions but is never practical and never completes her ambitions. No, she is not the precision processor, you would like her to be and is unable to complete your joint tax returns. Hence, you carry around a tiny distorted piece of her and this you worship on your altar to illusory love. The rest of the picture is far too tarnished and unsightly and not to your design and original specifications. You like to compare this fragment to Love's reality and claim they are the same. If only this were so! In the end, you compare a Love forever boundless, unconditional and free to one that is variable, demanding and exclusive. Equating one that blesses eternally with one that perpetually groans, and lives off sacrifice and endlessly engages in fierce battles of recrimination.

The ego laughs all the way to the bank. It is overjoyed with how you have been deceived, once again, by a form you like. It is delighted that you ignore the underlying content completely. Now you cannot win! For you have chosen to associate Love with the temporal, the bodily, and corruptible. You have therefore chosen death and remain firmly suckled on the nipples of illusion — Love's opposite in the dream. Now in your fear weakened condition, you know not where to turn. Your bondage and continued servitude are all-but guaranteed for you have hinged your dream of Love to a rust bucket, a fading flower, a voracious monstrosity, and a living nightmare. But what was the great offering that made you suck on the chocolate covered poison? What tempted you to ensnare yourself, once again in a dream of union, through exclusion? You cared not for the other, that is for sure but only for what you could extract from them. For false displays of passion, altruism and complete surrender are the double-dealing deceptions that underpin all special relationships.

Over time your specialness charades must become exposed for what they genuinely Are. An attempt at self-completion through pillaging and fleecing another. What is this but a vain attack on Truth fueled by the grandiosity of your ego. A pitiless misadventure to unearth the Home of Happiness and Peace in the unreal. That old ego ruse of *"Seek but do not*

Specialness: The Forbidden Fruit

find!" In the end, Humpty Dumpty must come crashing down and find you in despair because all special relationships are whacky endeavors to make exceptions to Love and still possess it. Only in holiness can you rediscover your strength. Use the world to make yourself special, and Truth must evade you. Each such relationship is an attempt to recover from your past failures and underlying feelings of lovelessness. You want to complete yourself by bringing the skeleton parade of pseudo-love out again and reliving these failed dynamics in the present.

Freud called special love, a narcissism of the mind and an aberrated form of self-love. It is the false jewel that seems to shine and glitter in the dark but seen in the light, its artificiality and shallowness are rapidly exposed. It may have delivered many beautiful reflections in the dream of the phenomenal world, but now its blemished edges and rusty core are beginning to show. No illusion of love can ever fulfill your heart's real desire. For that, an entirely new approach is called for. Many use special relationships as their hospital of salvation. A place to bandage themselves up to recover from their past. As a spiritual panacea for exhuming all those dark places in their mind where they felt downright pitiful in foregone times. Each represents an ego compensation in the dream. One that can be stuffed like a rag, to temporarily stop the bleeding.

Ultimately, we live and react through the lens of past events. All these psychodramas, we enact aim to divert our minds from living authentically in the present. Thus, we become self-relegated to living out our dream fantasies in a sad depot of the temporal. Often we use these relationships to take out vengeance on the past delivered to us. You see, we never genuinely accept nor embrace our real Selves. We hear only those cruel, deprecating words the ego continuously whispers into our ears. In the end, we do not uncompromisingly believe that we Are Love!

All the same, this moment experienced whole and complete is the only hospital needed for our healing and salvation. The special relationship is a toxic fountain of a twisted, convoluted love, ultimately sourced by our unconscious guilt. It is sought, only because we conceive of ourselves as unloving, frail, limited and housed in bodies. The ego uses this crown jewel to keep us hypnotized to a dream of earthly salvation. It does not attempt to heal the underlying notions of lovelessness that keeps us in prison. Its secret hope is for us to be dazzled by the beautiful frame that each special relationship offers and accept this in place of Love's Reality. Yes, it expects we will be lured and enchanted by the many glistening jewels of guilt, rage, and sin embedded in this frame and by all those illusions of love that stream at its periphery.

Specialness: The Forbidden Fruit

Will you continue to stand mesmerized by the gilded ornamental patterns engraved into this frame and thus be hoodwinked by the halo of illusory love that surrounds it?

The dream of specialness can only temporarily sedate your mind! As your life energy dissipates and trickles through a vast chasm of subterranean darkness, the only refreshment you will find is in those diaphanous mists of tears that fall gently upon your eyelids. Just long enough to avert your eyes from the many rivulets of blood cascading through the innermost part of the picture. Truly an abomination; you had unwittingly purchased in your sleep. These streams bear witness to your many tales of bitterness, misery, and regret and are used to help wash away the revolting stench of decaying bodies and all rottenness from the world. As you look a little closer, you see the great black hole of death at the center of the picture peering out, mocking you through sightless eyes. An infinity of men have gone into this well, never to return. All drowned in the inferno of the cosmic void. So will you continue to sip from the mirage of illusionary love or search instead for the Holy Grail to eternal life and unconditional Love? Only so will you know of that which never dies and can never fail.

Each special relationship embeds you deeper in time's stark manifold. Each consecrates specialness, the body and a hateful love as more worthy of your energy and time, than your unalterable holiness and perfection. The Holy Instant is Heaven's proven antidote for all forms of specialness esteemed by the dreaming mind. It comes to release you from the unreality of time and the festering ghetto of the body. Enter this Holy Portal but once and you will no longer entertain the shabby substitutes of the world in place of your immaculate Reality. Experiencing timelessness, even for an instant, hastens your plans and commitment to escape all bondage. Then you expeditiously dispossess all fetters of illusions and cross over the bridge into the Real world, never to look back.

Do not be fooled into considering special love and special hate, as polar opposites. In content, they are the same for they both share the same ego purpose of preserving guilt and separation. The special love relationship is a duplicitous ego attempt for retaining guilt by hiding it source deep inside your mind. The temptation of illusory love keeps all guilt densely screened from your active awareness and well hidden under a fortress of cunning defenses. You are taken in and seduced by the veneer of superficial love presented only at the surface.

Specialness: The Forbidden Fruit

Each special hate relationship is carefully forged and crafted in the cauldrons of existence so that it can be most efficaciously turned into a weapon against yourself. The ego slyly persuades that all the guilt and self-hate that is silently eating you can be eradicated through projection. So you deflect it to specific targets on the exterior. It will never clue you in on the real deal nor on the critical insight *"That all thought itself is spaceless."* The guilt can therefore never leave its source in your mind until there you release it. In the interim, you are being witlessly sold on an illusion of its displacement. Unless you voyage fearlessly within and surmise guilt's entire lack of foundation, there, it will never be dispelled. Alternatively, it can be released through your forgiveness of "others" and therefore by accepting forgiveness for yourself.

You must recognize the body, as an illusionary mind-generated barricade purposed with separating one part of your mind from another. The presence of the body makes you feel you can still successfully capture the special love denied to you by God. You foolishly imagine you can succeed in possessing Love by excluding parts of your mind while raising other aspects onto the pedestal. Without the body, your dream of specialness could not survive. As you relinquish your unwholesome desire in special love, your investment in the body begins to wane, paving the way for its eventual disappearance.

In the end, the cost of special love is far too steep for it demands the sacrifice of Love's Reality, to purchase an illusion. The repayment terms accrue interest that will yet be paid for in misery, isolation, alimony, tears, and bitterness. In special love, you attempt the death of God by erecting an idol in His place — an idol that mocks all who partake in its senseless charades. One that will fail all your heartfelt pleas and stipulations because it is built from the fabric of a dream. This icon you cherish so dearly just keeps you fast asleep in the Garden of Eden.

RECOGNIZING A SPECIAL RELATIONSHIP

How can we recognize a special relationship? Easily! Any relationship that rests on exclusion is a special one. This exclusion may be of another person, entire groups or just aspects of another's persona. Many clubs and organizations, for example, function more like cliques that are rampant hotbeds of cronyism and ego support. Members must meet certain exceptional requirements either of wealth, class, power, intelligence, privilege or connection to be able to join.

Most of these organizations are composed entirely of hateful, prejudicial folk, smeared with entitlement complexes. They rapidly become breathing grounds for all ego vices to proliferate. Often members will band together to form an outfit such as the Ku Klux Klan, the Aryan Brotherhood, the Crips, etc. whose motives are pretty transparent. The club is there to provide hate a safe-haven, and members oscillate between cultivating special love and hate relationships with it and each other. All of which is to be expected from fractured individuals with highly distortionary beliefs. Such hate filled organizations cannot even embrace a complete ego in its entirety but insist on making rules, demanding respect and badgering its members to do reprehensible deeds.

They often will not tolerate the addictive, power hungry and controlling natures of those prone to join. Their membership consists of many forceful personalities who abhor external subjugation but who recognize the need for forming collaborative alliances to act out their hate. After all the mob mentality provides a buffer of protection, and it can accomplish so much more than any sole individual working alone. Nevertheless, unless such individuals align with the organization's prime passion for terrorizing the weak, they will be swiftly isolated and lose all privileges. Then placed in a bubble, where they will be scrutinized, interrogated, ostracized or even murdered.

They are plenty of organizations like this permeating the dark underground of our society; groups dedicated to attracting fringe outliers of the worst sort. They adore those already poisoned by various vices and insecurities since these are very malleable beings and easily manipulated into endorsing group ideologies. A bonus is that most already hold the seeds of their self-destruction and have nothing much to lose. All of which aptly demonstrate why ego alliances are always tenuous, fractious and unstable.

Special love relationships are essentially paradoxical in their essence since even so-called loving couples spend most of their time engaging in ego lashing wars. That doting love which was there, after a good fuck in the morning has suddenly transformed into a monstrous beast of hate by mid-afternoon. A vile creature with horns now emerges from the upstairs bedroom; one spitting venom and fire in all directions as it randomly flails about the house searching for the next character flaw upon which to alight and devour. What trivial piece of minutiae can it focus upon next to justify its rage? The hissing match may continue well into the night. What remains constant, is the ego and its unholy aspiration to worship specialness and exclusion in place of holiness and inclusion. This unfortunate framework bars any real union and calls out for an endless chain of deceptions and callous attacks. All of which becomes the perfect environment for shutting Love out. In its makeup, the relationship is an insidious nest of hell and fury because what is hell but a state of mind where Love can never enter.

Special love and hate relationships deny the underlying guilt and insecurity which motivates their formation. They are plea bargain bids made by the ego to negotiate and strike a deal with Love, in the name of idolatry. Meanwhile, the guilt at their core along with all feelings of incompletion and worthlessness are carefully concealed and pushed deeper underground. Even so, the real hate and evil continue, lurking just below the surface, ready to be remembered at the tiniest insult. In the special love relationship, we see all the shady contracts, bribes and guilt alleviation games. The flimsy, superficial love bubble can so easily be burst, in an instant. Then the real terrifying face of the relationship is witnessed, and the absence of any genuine loving content becomes overwhelmingly evident. From then on the beasts of psychic warfare, overt savagery and perfidious intent roam the landscape of perception unchecked.

> **"Recognize this, for it is true, and truth must be recognized if it is to be distinguished from illusion: The special love relationship is an attempt to bring love into separation. And, as such, it is nothing more than an attempt to bring love into fear, and make it real in fear. In fundamental violation of love's one condition, the**

special love relationship would accomplish the impossible."

[ACIM, T-16.IV.7:1-3]

Special love relationships are protected "paradises" in the relative world where the ego can play its games of make-believe and shadowy pretense. In such protected havens, it can continue to entertain the foolish notion, that it can be truly loving. Such relationships may contain some flattery, consideration, and affection at times, but never Love. Each remains an attractive form of fear wrapped in an alluring package that deceives. Each offers the illusion of heaven while masking its true content from all conscious awareness. Even so, each would retain no power to conceal its essential nature and purpose were it not for your attraction to guilt.

Each is born out of your need for special love, denied to you by God. You seek to raise the other on the pedestal while simultaneously reducing yourself into insignificance. You then engage in countless self-mortifications or become a living death in the vain hope that you can make your idol shine all the more brightly. Having assessed yourself as virtually worthless, hateful and repulsive, you gladly sell your bag of bones on the altar of illusory love to purchase the soul of another. There is a trading of self-concepts in which you die to the self-concept you formerly esteemed of yourself only to be reborn in the glowing concept you now hold of another.

Such relationships are temptations placed in your path by the ego to have you settle for illusion in place of Truth. Meanwhile, it casually dismisses the pearl of priceless value found only in the Holy relationship. These bonds of false intimacy are only attractive to those who already feel diminutive and deprived. They charm and seduce those who possess a scarcity consciousness, having lost sight of their Heavenly grandeur. Each is an attempt to carve out a little happiness from that mud-pit of insanity and meaninglessness in which you feel embalmed. The body becomes the altar to be decorated and adorned and promoted as the ego's chosen vehicle for exclusion. All the jewels, glorifying rags and flowers you garland it with, promise to exalt it sufficiently so that you can snare some living bait. Thus you trap your prize into this hopeless refuge that you pretend is a rejuvenating sanctuary and healing oasis. Nonetheless, all that these measures do is instantiate false hope because they deny the relationship is a crumbling castle ready to be torn down and condemned. Can a bag of dust surrounding a core of rust uncover the glory of the eternal and the enduring radiance of the unconditionally loving?

Specialness: The Forbidden Fruit

Meanwhile, you exploit these alliances also for attack and indulgence and to mitigate your deep-seated rage and unhappiness at existence. Enmeshed in this twisted cloud and reality distortion field of your projected narcissism your senses become bewitched. In your blindness, fear becomes the determiner of when is the right moment to pounce. And so like a Knight Templar you head out to conquer the armies of the dark ones hoping to gain at last some measure of retribution for the many cruelties inflicted in the past. Mission accomplished, the ego relaxes and loosens the reigns so that you can luxuriate in the pleasure caves and go positively bonkers and mindless, for a while. So soon you are seen stumbling about the ghettoes and opium dens of the world behaving like a mad cow while drinking the ambrosia nectar. Stupefied beyond measure and hypnotically bound to the dream of time and fantasy, you resemble a zombified goon hopelessly navigating its lunar landing module across psychoplanet.

The central theme and assertion of each special relationship is that the illusion of love can be made satisfying. God must first be expunged from all conscious thought so that you can thoroughly enjoy your games of denial. Love, by its very nature, is wholly without fear, yet each such collaboration is so replete with fear and mistrust. **Unconditional Love does not change nor vacillate with time.** We see, however, that the love offered in the special relationship is fickle, acrimonious, hateful, sacrificial and brimming with guilt. Hence it leads speedily to all modes of disillusionment, self-destruction and even despair.

The special relationship holds you to this side of paradise. Since it binds you to the dream of the relative existence, it secures your faith in the ephemeral. Realize, on this side of the bridge, is nothing sacred and lasting. Nothing but that kaleidoscopic parade of fleeting pleasures and idols with no life-giving breath. All is strategically designed to keep your senses fettered to the temples of indulgence and the pleasure pits of vice. The orgiastic Dionysian Gods of the Inner Sanctum are prostrated to, as you rapidly devolve into a shameless voluptuary dedicated to transient gratifications. Your mind becomes so chained to the gutter that you become unable to break free and heal.

Your only hope is in transforming each into a Holy one. This reversal of purpose is the Holy Spirit's answer and solution, and it marks a fundamental shift in the relationship's content and operating dynamic. The goal now becomes Heaven. A mission which restores perfect Love to your awareness. Full advantage is taken of Holy Instants to heal the relationship and to go past all ego illusions that captivated and hypnotized in the past. You begin to embrace the other in their totality and recognize the face of Spirit in all. As you vaporize the dense cloud of the unreal, you penetrate to the other's original face. Glimpsing his innate and unalterable perfection and underlying holiness, you awaken from all time-based dreams. The pathetic, failing and sinful image that was perceived before cannot last long once illuminated under the light of your newfound vision.

Such is salvation's remedy to all the havoc wreaked by the special relationship. It is a sound and workable solution which obliterates all the pain, deception and fear-based manipulation and control. In the Holy relationship, the real meaning of freedom and Love becomes known. No one must die so that another can live; no one must lose so that all can gain. The acknowledgment of Holiness anywhere heals us all as one. The Holy Relationship is truly one of Love without strings, and it presents a welcome, restful and inviting Abode, in which health and Peace are finally restored, and ego wars are no more!

3. Radiant Thoughts

Being aware that holiness is the Heavenly Answer to all the ego's quests for specialness, you may be ready to digest a few more powerful insights. Firstly, we are accustomed to considering our thoughts as being of more or less the same order of reality. This ideation is pure nonsense! One perpetuated by the voice of insanity within who is incapable of Knowledge.

Specialness: The Forbidden Fruit

All our thoughts fall into two fundamental classifications that are worlds apart. They will embody Truth or Falsehood and therefore will be real or unreal. In our profound state of confusion and ignorance, we can no longer distinguish our real thoughts from our unreal ones. This world-changing insight holds true also for our experiences. And so our experiences can be both Real and Unreal. For example, when you are experiencing an hallucination, it is an acutely unreal experience and perception. One unshared by all other aspects of mind. Nevertheless, your mind in its severely misguided state does not recognize it as such. In contrast, the experience of Revelations is an overwhelmingly real experience and one communicated unambiguously from the sphere of purity, timelessness, and truth. Revelatory experiences are nonsymbolic and wordless communications because symbols and words always distort to some degree. The bulk of our experiences are predominantly only partially true. They will reflect truth to varying degrees from the extreme of an almost perfect reflection to that dim penumbra of Self-obscuring rubbish.

All our perceptual experiences contain elements and aspects that distort. Holy Instants are examples of experiences that weigh forcibly on the side of Truth. They are Truth communicated symbolically and in its least distorted form into the realm of the Relative. You may wonder at this point, "**How can I distinguish my Real from my Unreal Thoughts?**" There are definitely very defined criteria for doing very easily and effectively. I will now emphasize some of the most important:

1. *Real Thoughts Never Vacillate in Their Message.*

2. *Real Thoughts Only Bring Joy.*

3. *Real Thoughts Empower and Liberate.*

4. *Real Thoughts Always Heal and Integrate the Mind.*

1. Real Thoughts Never Vacillate in Their Message

Anything sourced from the Kingdom of Truth never changes or fluctuates in its message. The potent but invisible content which Real Thoughts impart is not subject to the vagaries and distortions of Time. What is certain, does not need to change. In fact, it is impossible for it to do so and retain its certitude. It is only the conditional that ever changes. This unflappable constancy which Real Thoughts embody is found very reassuring to the mind. It brings it joy and healing.

For example, the Thought "**God IS!**" is a Real Thought. It represents a thought that can only be quantized into a "**1**" or a "**0**", or as either "**True**" or "**Untrue**"; A statement that leaves no room for compromise or bargains in-between. Either God exists, or He does not. He cannot be partially true since His existence is Total or Void. The Real Thought "**God IS**" carries the happy message that His Being is True and this never alters or changes. He is always present and in all things.

2. Real Thoughts Only Bring Joy

Their message is a positive one that never changes. The hidden content, encapsulated within each Real Thought can be relied upon under all circumstances. Just as a dog gives its owner unconditional love, Real Thoughts bestow unconditional joy. Ambiguous messages and those that change daily are what produce all misery and fear. The mind finds no calm center where it can rest before being forced to move on. Instead, it perpetually feels like a homeless vagabond is an unwelcoming and hostile realm. Even though it is pressured to move from one park bench or temporary shelter to another, it never finds an enduring place of rest where it can relax at last. For example, consider the following Real Thought.

"I am the Eternal, Limitless and All-powerful Son of God who rests safely and in Peace high above the Kingdom of Illusion."

If you knew to this to be true with the full conviction of your Being, just think how much joy it would release into your mind. No phantom of the Relative World would hold any power over you then. None would have the capacity to disturb or diminish your unassailable peace. Your Home is never going to be sent into foreclosure or ever be taken away. Even Death cannot accomplish such a feat because death, itself, is also just an illusion whose power extends only to the body. Death holds not an ounce of sway in the realm of the Eternal and true. Its credentials and jurisdiction cannot extend that far because it can never rise above the illusory. Being Eternal, you are not subject to sickness or suffering or any other bodily thoughts. Such deities only hold power and influence and rise to confuse whenever you temporarily identify with the illusory. Their presence is always the consequence of having lost access to your Real Thoughts.

3. Real Thoughts Empower and Liberate

Certainty is power. But there are two types of certainty. **(1)** The **blind certainty** of the unquestioning, ignorant and closed-minded and **(2)** The **Calm, Lucid Certainty** of those who have reached to Wisdom and Perfect Knowledge.

The first type of certainty is critically flawed because of all its hidden fears and failures to question and interrogate its autogenous knowledge. The second, in contrast, is integrated, stable and serene because it finds no need to question anymore. Those who have reached the pinnacle of Knowledge and understanding have successfully vaporized all errors, distortions, and contradictions that could serve to introduce any confusion and doubt. From their extremely elevated and otherworldly position, all paths lead downward. They find no need to entertain any worldly, relative or conditional thought or ideation since this would just be diluting and contaminating with illusions and impurities, their incontrovertible Knowledge.

Specialness: The Forbidden Fruit

Those who gratify and cherish illusions move through time while those who have disbanded all illusions, through pure insight and reason are illuminated and enter the timeless. In-between these two extremes, the mind is always on the move. Jesus communicated how this world is but a bridge; we should pass over but not seek to build a home upon. There can be no joyful, stable home that endures in the Relative World.

The wisest path to take, for those who have not yet reached the certainty of perfect Knowledge is that of open-mindedness and uncertainty. **Uncertainty is the path to wisdom just as unwarranted certainty is the path that leads down into that dark nebulous realm of further bondage**. As one migrates and navigates along the path of uncertainty, Real Thoughts serve as the light-bearers that empower and direct to freedom.

4. Real Thoughts Always Heal and Integrate the Mind

In the final analysis, only Truth can heal! All other remedies are temporary and superficial, by nature because they extend to the realm of the non-existent. They cannot be said to be true and lasting cures in any real sense because they incarnate no unfading power. Spells of the mind is a better word for them. Worldly remedies and "cures" are spells that temporarily seduce the mind. They are forms of black magic and magical solution which the mind endorses and becomes intoxicated upon, being unwilling or unable to find the Source of healing light within.

Real Thoughts, being in harmony with Truth retain the power to heal your mind completely. One Real Thought is sufficient because all are linked seamlessly and share a singular content. Healing is integration just is sickness arises from increased dissociation which then automatically brings disconnection and further isolation. It is in this well of darkness that all illusions flower. From here they rise in a hostile takeover to take complete command of the mind.

SOME MORE EXAMPLES OF REAL THOUGHTS

My Salvation Is Guaranteed, By God!

I am the Immaculate Awareness, in which All Things Appear to Happen!

The Body, Sickness, and Death are all just Appearances in the lower mind.

Heaven IS! It is this world that has Never Been!

When All Dreams no longer Tempt me, Truth will Shine Outward from my Mind!

Truth Remains Always Relevant.

I Am As God Created Me! Not as I made Myself!

AUTHOR BIO

Sharon Moriarty is a Yogi, Mystic, and Adventurer. In her past lives, she professionally engaged in Hardware Engineering, Management, Lecturing, Software Development, and Sales. She enjoys sharing her insights and wisdom on the Course material and communicating its ideas in a very lucid and in-depth manner. She hopes you enjoy and progress rapidly on your Spiritual journey.

OTHER BOOKS BY SHARON MORIARTY

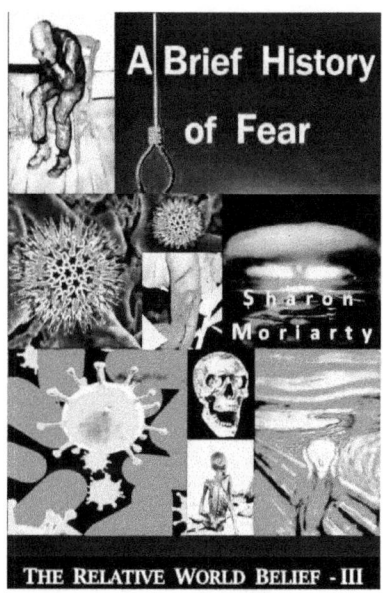

E-Books and Paperbacks Available now on Amazon and CreateSpace.

http://www.Amazon.com

www.ingramcontent.com/pod-product-compliance
Lightning Source LLC
Chambersburg PA
CBHW071328040426
42444CB00009B/2107